8/15

THE GREATEST RECORDS IN SPORTS

HOCKEY'S
GREATEST RECORDS

Katie Kawa

PowerKiDS
press.

New York

Published in 2015 by The Rosen Publishing Group, Inc.
29 East 21st Street, New York, NY 10010

First Edition

Editor: Katie Kawa
Book Design: Reann Nye

Library of Congress Cataloging-in-Publication Data

Kawa, Katie.
Hockey's greatest records / by Katie Kawa.
p. cm. — (The greatest records in sports)
Includes index.
ISBN 978-1-4994-0236-0 (pbk.)
ISBN 978-1-4994-0180-6 (6-pack)
ISBN 978-1-4994-0228-5 (library binding)
1. Hockey — Records — United States — Juvenile literature. 2. Hockey — Records — Canada — Juvenile literature. 3. National Hockey League — Juvenile literature. I. Kawa, Katie. II. Title.
GV847.5 K3918 2015
796.962—d23

Manufactured in the United States of America

CPSIA Compliance Information: Batch #CW15PK: For Further Information contact Rosen Publishing, New York, New York at 1-800-237-9932

CONTENTS

THE HISTORY OF HOCKEY

Sports fans compare athletes using their **statistics**, or stats. Statistics show who holds records in a sport, including the most goals, points, and wins. Sports records are held by some of the greatest athletes in history, and the history of hockey is filled with talented record holders.

Hockey is one of the most popular winter sports in the world. People have been playing the sport as we know it today for over 150 years! Canada is known as the birthplace of hockey, which began as an outdoor activity. The first recorded hockey game played on an indoor rink took place in Montreal, Canada, on March 3, 1875. Since then, hockey games have been played everywhere from Olympic rinks in Russia to outdoor football **stadiums** in the United States.

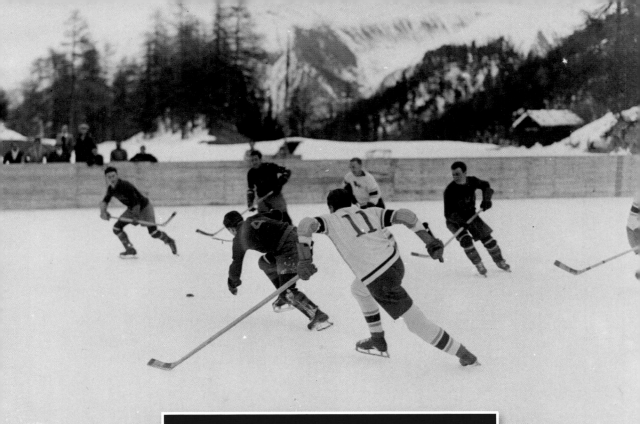

Although hockey began in Canada, it's also a popular sport in the United States. The National Hockey League (NHL) is made up of teams from both Canada and the United States.

THE HOCKEY HALL OF FAME

The greatest hockey players in the sport's long history are **inducted** into the Hockey Hall of Fame in Toronto, Canada. Each year, a special selection **committee** votes on who belongs in the Hockey Hall of Fame. Statistics play a big part in deciding who gets inducted.

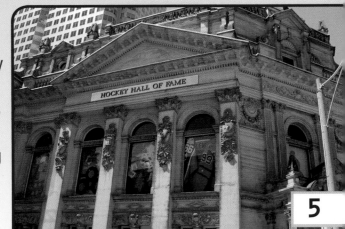

THE GREAT ONE

The winning team in a hockey game is the team that scores the most goals. Often, the players who score the most goals are the most famous. Goals are scored by shooting the puck into the other team's net. This isn't an easy task because the shooter has to get the puck past the other team's goalie. Hockey games are often low-scoring games for this reason.

Hockey players called forwards often score the most goals. It's their job to move forward up the ice to try to score. The most successful forward in hockey history is Wayne Gretzky. He holds many scoring records, including the most goals scored in a career.

SUPERIOR STATS
MOST GOALS IN A CAREER

PLAYER	GOALS	YEAR INDUCTED INTO HOCKEY HALL OF FAME
WAYNE GRETZKY	894	1999
GORDIE HOWE	801	1972
BRETT HULL	741	2009
MARCEL DIONNE	731	1992
PHIL ESPOSITO	717	1984

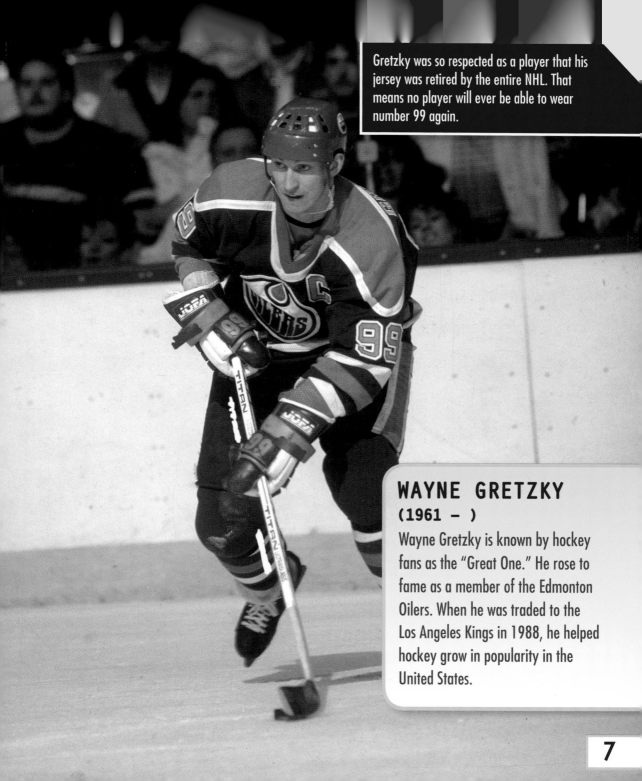

Gretzky was so respected as a player that his jersey was retired by the entire NHL. That means no player will ever be able to wear number 99 again.

WAYNE GRETZKY
(1961 –)

Wayne Gretzky is known by hockey fans as the "Great One." He rose to fame as a member of the Edmonton Oilers. When he was traded to the Los Angeles Kings in 1988, he helped hockey grow in popularity in the United States.

Gretzky holds many other hockey records, too, such as the most goals scored in one season. During the 1981–1982 season, Gretzky scored 92 goals for the Oilers. That's an average of more than one goal per game. You can find the average goals per game a player has scored by diving their total number of goals by the number of games they played.

Sometimes a hockey player scores more than one goal in a game. This is rare! When a player scores three goals in a game, it's called a hat trick. Gretzky scored more hat tricks than any other player. He had 50 of them in his career.

SUPERIOR STATS
MOST HAT TRICKS IN A CAREER

PLAYER	HAT TRICKS
WAYNE GRETZKY	50
MARIO LEMIEUX	40
MIKE BOSSY	39
BRETT HULL	33
PHIL ESPOSITO	32

Mario Lemieux

When a player scores a hat trick, fans often throw their hats on the ice to celebrate. Mario Lemieux, a forward for the Pittsburgh Penguins, scored the second-highest number of hat tricks in a career, with 40.

PASSING THE PUCK

A hockey player doesn't often score a goal without help from at least one teammate. When a player passes the puck to a player who scores a goal, that's called an assist. Up to two players can be **awarded** assists on a goal in the NHL.

Passing plays in hockey often happen between the two different types of forwards: the center and wingers. The center plays between the left winger and the right winger.

Gretzky was a center, and he also holds the record for the most career assists, with 1,963. The player behind him on the all-time assists list, Ron Francis, was also a center. Centers generally do more skating than players at any other position. They have more freedom than wingers.

RON FRANCIS
(1963–)

Ron Francis was one of the best passing centers to ever play in the NHL. He's also known as a great leader. He was the captain of both the Hartford Whalers and Pittsburgh Penguins at different times during his career. Francis was inducted into the Hockey Hall of Fame in 2007.

Hockey players who have a large number of assists, such as Francis, are good at finding other players on the ice. They practice their passing skills often to stay at their best.

SUPERIOR STATS
MOST CAREER ASSISTS

PLAYER	ASSISTS
WAYNE GRETZKY	1,963
RON FRANCIS	1,249
MARK MESSIER	1,193
RAYMOND BOURQUE	1,169
PAUL COFFEY	1,135

COMBINING STATS

One way to show a player's overall offensive success during his NHL career is to combine statistics. For example, a hockey player is said to have scored a point when they record either a goal or an assist. Altogether, a player's total number of goals and assists equals the player's total points.

Points show how good a player is at both passing and scoring. Gretzky was the best at both because he's the NHL leader in career points, with 2,857. The next player on the list, Mark Messier, has almost 1,000 fewer points. This shows just how **dominant** Gretzky was when he played. That's how he became known as the "Great One"!

SUPERIOR STATS
MOST CAREER POINTS

PLAYER	GOALS	ASSISTS	POINTS
WAYNE GRETZKY	894	1,963	2,857
MARK MESSIER	694	1,193	1,887
GORDIE HOWE	801	1,049	1,850
RON FRANCIS	549	1,249	1,798
MARCEL DIONNE	731	1,040	1,771

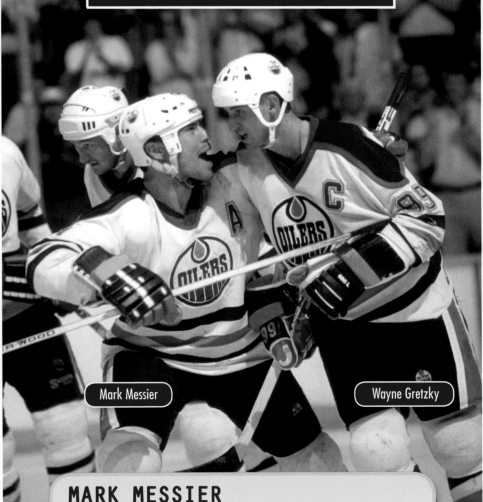

Gretzky and Messier were teammates with the Oilers, and together they helped their team win four championships.

Mark Messier

Wayne Gretzky

MARK MESSIER
(1961–)

Mark Messier is known for much more than just his ability to score points. He's one of the most respected players in NHL history because of his leadership. Messier was the first player to be the captain of two championship-winning NHL teams from different cities: the Oilers in 1990 and the New York Rangers in 1994.

TO THE BOX!

Hockey is a game filled with hard hits and even some fights. There are rules in place to protect players and to keep teams from unfairly scoring or preventing the other team from scoring. Teams are punished for breaking rules by receiving a penalty. When a penalty is called against a player, they're sent to the penalty box, and their team must play with one fewer player for a set number of minutes. This is called playing shorthanded.

Penalties are recorded in minutes. Sometimes teams purposely get penalties because they believe it gives the players a spark of energy. This often happens when two players fight each other. Both players in the fight get a five-minute penalty. On March 5, 2004, a game between the Ottawa Senators and Philadelphia Flyers set an NHL record with 419 penalty minutes!

If a penalty occurs on certain clear-scoring chances, the team trying to score is awarded a penalty shot. During a penalty shot, a player gets a chance to score with only the goalie in the way.

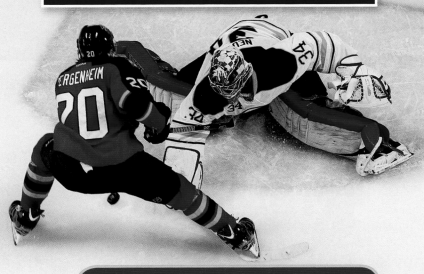

SUPERIOR STATS
MOST CAREER
PENALTY MINUTES

PLAYER	PENALTIES (IN MINUTES)
TIGER WILLIAMS	3,966
DALE HUNTER	3,565
TIE DOMI	3,515
MARTY MCSORLEY	3,381
BOB PROBERT	3,300

TYPES OF PENALTIES

Some penalties in hockey are worse than others. If a player trips another player, they get a two-minute minor penalty. Fighting is a five-minute major penalty. If a player tries to **injure** another player, they're given a game misconduct. They're **ejected** from the game, but their team doesn't have to play shorthanded.

POWER-PLAY PERFORMERS

When a team is playing shorthanded, the other team is said to be on a power play. Most power plays feature five players against four, but sometimes two penalties are called against one team. In those cases, the power play becomes what's known as a 5-on-3.

A power play for a minor penalty lasts two minutes, but it also ends if the team on the power play scores. Passing is very important to success on a power play. The power play is often controlled by the players at the point, or the top of the offensive zone. These players sometimes score on hard, swinging shots at the goal, or slap shots. Other times, these shots are tipped into the goal by players right in front of the net.

DAVE ANDREYCHUK (1963–)

Dave Andreychuk holds the record for most power-play goals in a career. He began his NHL career with the Buffalo Sabres. He later won a championship with the Tampa Bay Lightning, and he's one of only four players to score 30 or more power-play goals in one season.

Dave Andreychuk scored more power-play goals than any other NHL player, with 274. On the other hand, Gretzky scored the most shorthanded goals, with 73. These are goals scored when the other team has a power play.

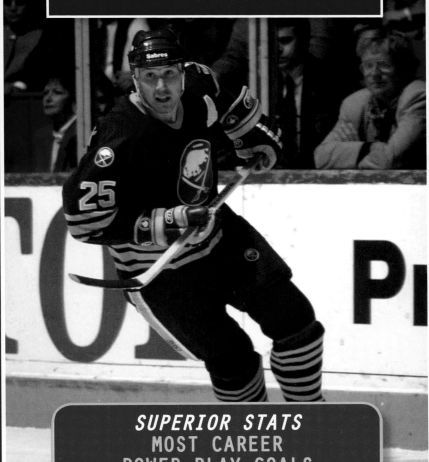

SUPERIOR STATS
MOST CAREER POWER-PLAY GOALS

PLAYER	POWER-PLAY GOALS
DAVE ANDREYCHUK	274
BRETT HULL	265
TEEMU SELANNE	255
PHIL ESPOSITO	249
LUC ROBITAILLE	247

While a forward's job in the NHL is to score goals, a defenseman's job is to keep the other team from scoring. Defensemen do this by forcing the other team's forwards to the outer edges of the rink, which keeps them from getting a clear shot at the goal. They also keep the other team's players from getting to the front of their net and tipping a puck past their goalie.

BOBBY ORR
(1948–)

Bobby Orr changed the game of hockey forever by showing that defensemen could also be great scorers. During the 1970–1971 NHL season, he recorded 139 points. That set a single-season scoring record for defensemen that has yet to be broken. Orr was inducted into the Hockey Hall of Fame in 1979.

Forwards have to help the defensemen by covering the other team's players when the puck is near their goal. Defensemen can help forwards, too, by scoring goals. Defensemen don't score often, but some become famous for their scoring ability. Raymond Bourque has the record for most goals (410) and points (1,579) by a defenseman in his career.

Bobby Orr won the Norris **Trophy**, given to the NHL's best defenseman each season, eight times in a row!

SUPERIOR STATS
MOST CAREER GOALS BY A DEFENSEMAN

PLAYER	GOALS
RAYMOND BOURQUE	410
PAUL COFFEY	396
AL MACINNIS	340
PHIL HOUSLEY	338
DENIS POTVIN	310

PLUS PLAYERS

One statistic used to measure the abilities of both forwards and defensive players is plus-minus rating. All players who are on the ice when their team scores earn a "plus." The only kind of goal that doesn't count toward a "plus" is a power-play goal. A player is given a "minus" if they're on the ice when the other team scores any goal except a power-play goal. The difference between these numbers is a player's plus-minus rating.

Plus-minus ratings can be **negative** or positive numbers. A negative plus-minus rating means a player is having trouble both offensively and defensively. A positive plus-minus rating means the player is good at both parts of the game. Larry Robinson's record plus-minus rating for his career is 730!

LARRY ROBINSON
(1951–)

Larry Robinson started his NHL career with the Montreal Canadiens in 1971. He was part of some of the most famous and talented teams in hockey history, playing in 227 **playoff** games during his 20-year career. He retired with 958 career points and became a member of the Hockey Hall of Fame in 1995.

These players all received a "plus" for being on the ice when a goal was scored for their team. Robinson must have been a part of a lot of celebrations like this one!

SUPERIOR STATS
CAREER PLUS-MINUS RATING

PLAYER	POSITION	PLUS-MINUS RATING
LARRY ROBINSON	DEFENSEMAN	730
BOBBY ORR	DEFENSEMAN	597
RAYMOND BOURQUE	DEFENSEMAN	528
WAYNE GRETZKY	CENTER	518
BOBBY CLARKE	CENTER	506

GREAT GOALIES

The last line of defense for a hockey team is the goalie. It's the goalie's job to stop the puck from getting into the net.

If a team wins a game, the goalie who was on the ice for that game records a statistic called a win. Goalies with many wins are very good at their job, and they often play on teams that are very good, too. A strong defense helps make a goalie's job easier. Goalies with many wins also play for many seasons.

Martin Brodeur holds the record for the most career wins by a goalie. By the end of the 2013–2014 season, he had 688 wins. However, he's still an active player in the NHL. His record number of wins could go even higher as he keeps playing.

SUPERIOR STATS
MOST CAREER WINS
(AS OF 2013–2014 SEASON)

GOALIE	WINS
MARTIN BRODEUR*	688
PATRICK ROY	551
ED BELFOUR	484
CURTIS JOSEPH	454
TERRY SAWCHUK	447

* = active goalie

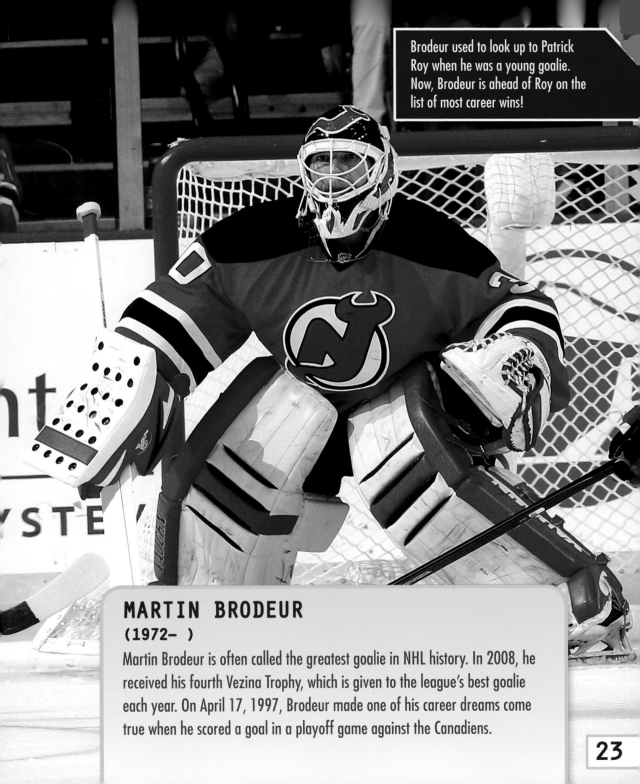

Brodeur used to look up to Patrick Roy when he was a young goalie. Now, Brodeur is ahead of Roy on the list of most career wins!

MARTIN BRODEUR
(1972–)

Martin Brodeur is often called the greatest goalie in NHL history. In 2008, he received his fourth Vezina Trophy, which is given to the league's best goalie each year. On April 17, 1997, Brodeur made one of his career dreams come true when he scored a goal in a playoff game against the Canadiens.

Sometimes a goalie plays so well that the other team doesn't score a goal for the entire game. This is called a shutout. A team's defensive game must also be very strong for a shutout to occur. Although hockey is a low-scoring game, shutouts don't happen very often.

Brodeur also holds the record for most shutouts. As of the end of the 2013–2014 season, he had recorded 124 of them. That number could go up as he keeps playing.

Brodeur's style of goaltending has helped him **achieve** his success. It's a mix of different styles, and it often confuses shooters from other teams. One of his best methods for stopping the puck is using his glove to catch it.

SUPERIOR STATS
MOST CAREER SHUTOUTS
(AS OF 2013–2014 SEASON)

GOALIE	SHUTOUTS
MARTIN BRODEUR*	124
TERRY SAWCHUK	103
GEORGE HAINSWORTH	94
GLENN HALL	84
JACQUES PLANTE	82

* = active player

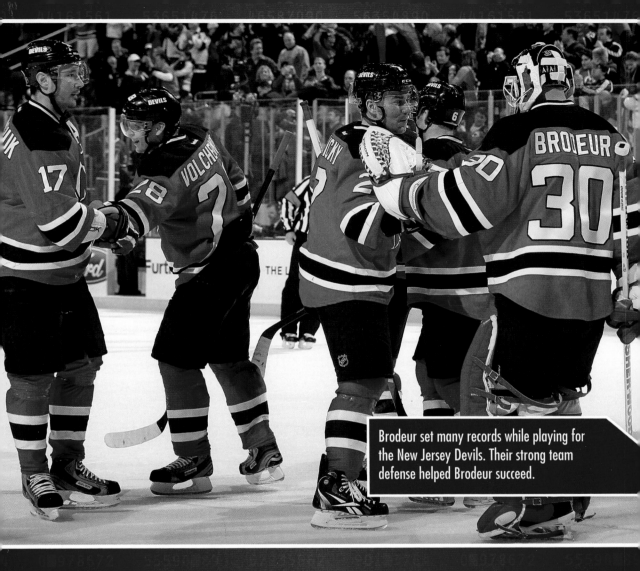

Brodeur set many records while playing for the New Jersey Devils. Their strong team defense helped Brodeur succeed.

STYLES OF GOALTENDING

Brodeur's style is a cross between the butterfly style of goaltending and the stand-up style. Butterfly goalies drop to their knees to make most of their saves. The pads on their legs then look like butterfly wings. Stand-up goalies do most their work on their skates.

THE STANLEY CUP

The Stanley Cup is the trophy given to the champions of the NHL every year. It was first used as a trophy in 1893. Today, it's become one of the most famous trophies in **professional** sports.

The Stanley Cup isn't easy to win. The NHL playoffs, which are often called the Stanley Cup Playoffs, are four rounds long. In each round, teams play a set of games called a series. The first team to win four games in a series moves on to the next round.

Some teams have never won the Stanley Cup, but others have won the trophy many times. The record for most Stanley Cup Championships is held by the Montreal Canadiens, with 24 as of the 2013–2014 season.

HENRI RICHARD
(1936–)

Henri Richard won more Stanley Cups than any other player in the history of the NHL. Richard was born in Montreal, Quebec, on February 29, 1936. He began playing in the NHL in 1955, and his career lasted 20 years! During that time, he won 11 Stanley Cups.

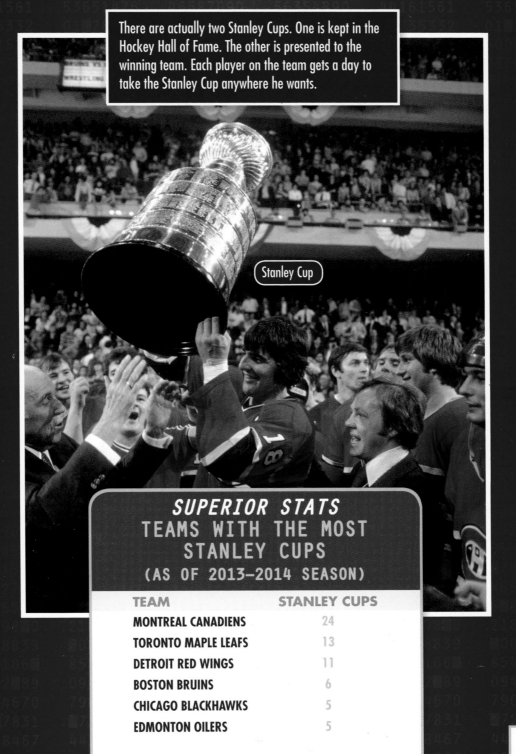

There are actually two Stanley Cups. One is kept in the Hockey Hall of Fame. The other is presented to the winning team. Each player on the team gets a day to take the Stanley Cup anywhere he wants.

Stanley Cup

SUPERIOR STATS
TEAMS WITH THE MOST STANLEY CUPS
(AS OF 2013–2014 SEASON)

TEAM	STANLEY CUPS
MONTREAL CANADIENS	24
TORONTO MAPLE LEAFS	13
DETROIT RED WINGS	11
BOSTON BRUINS	6
CHICAGO BLACKHAWKS	5
EDMONTON OILERS	5

WOMEN'S HOCKEY RECORDS

Hockey is a sport that both men and women play. Women's hockey is rising in popularity around the world, and many high schools and colleges in the United States now have women's hockey teams.

Women's hockey was included in the Olympics for the first time in 1998. The United States won the first gold medal in the sport, but Canada has the record for most gold medals. In 2014, Canada won its fourth women's hockey gold medal.

JULIE CHU
(1982–)

Julie Chu is one of only three women's hockey players to play for the United States in four Olympics. She graduated from Harvard University in 2007. Chu was chosen to carry the U.S. flag during the closing **ceremonies** of the 2014 Olympics, which is a very high honor for an Olympic athlete.

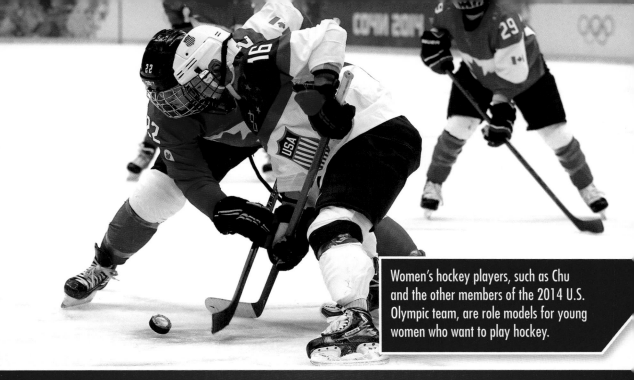

Women's hockey players, such as Chu and the other members of the 2014 U.S. Olympic team, are role models for young women who want to play hockey.

As women's hockey continues to grow in popularity, more and more young girls are starting to pick up skates and sticks. A whole new group of future record holders is getting ready to show hockey fans what they can do!

SUPERIOR STATS
MOST TEAM USA OLYMPIC APPEARANCES
(AS OF 2014)

PLAYER	POSITION	OLYMPICS
JULIE CHU	DEFENSE/FORWARD	4 (2002, 2006, 2010, 2014)
JENNY POTTER	FORWARD	4 (1998, 2002, 2006, 2010)
ANGELA RUGGIERO	DEFENSE	4 (1998, 2002, 2006, 2010)
NATALIE DARWITZ	FORWARD	3 (2002, 2006, 2010)
TRICIA DUNN-LUOMA	FORWARD	3 (1998, 2002, 2006)
KATIE KING	FORWARD	3 (1998, 2002, 2006)

The Hockey Hall of Fame is filled with record holders, and today's best players are chasing their records. Patrick Kane, Sidney Crosby, and Alexander Ovechkin are just three of the many current stars looking to leave their mark on the NHL like the greats who came before them.

The holders of hockey's greatest records achieved success through hard work. Their stories teach young hockey players—whether they're boys or girls—what it takes to be the best in their sport. The best players of hockey's past and present have set a good example for the future stars of the sport.

GLOSSARY

achieve: To get by effort.

award: To give something good.

ceremony: A formal act done in a certain way to honor a special occasion.

committee: A group of people chosen to consider or take action on some matter.

dominant: Better than all others.

eject: To throw out by authority.

induct: To admit or bring in as a member.

injure: To hurt.

negative: Less than zero.

playoff: A game that's played after the regular season to determine which teams will play for a sport's championship.

professional: Having to do with a job someone does for a living.

stadium: A large, commonly outdoor building where people gather to watch sporting events.

statistic: A number that stands for a piece of information.

trophy: An object given to honor an accomplishment.

INDEX

WEBSITES

Due to the changing nature of Internet links, PowerKids Press has developed an online list of websites related to the subject of this book. This site is updated regularly. Please use this link to access the list: www.powerkidslinks.com/gris/hoc